THE ARCTIC LAND

Bobbie Kalman

The Arctic World Series

Crabtree Publishing Company

The Arctic World Series
Created by Bobbie Kalman

Editor-in-Chief:
Bobbie Kalman

Writing team:
Bobbie Kalman
Janine Schaub
Liz Hart
Christine Arthurs
Ken Faris

Managing Editor:
Janine Schaub

Editors:
Liz Hart
Christine Arthurs
Tilly Crawley

Maps:
Chrismar Mapping Services Inc.

Design:
Heather Delfino
Maureen Shaughnessy
Stephen Latimer

Computer layout:
Christine Arthurs

For Julie and Joel

Special thanks to: Ken Faris for his groundwork in the series; Joel Mercer for his expert geographical advice; Berit Qundos for tracking down photos in Stockholm; Robin Brass for his desktop publishing advice and linotronic output; Arnie Krause for his continuing patience and support.

Gift 7/12

Cataloguing in Publication Data

Kalman, Bobbie, 1947-
    The Arctic Land

(The Arctic world series)
Includes index.
ISBN 0-86505-144-5 (bound) ISBN 0-86505-154-2 (pbk.)

1. Arctic regions - Juvenile literature. 2. Arctic races - Arctic regions - Juvenile literature. 3. Natural history - Arctic regions - Juvenile literature. 4. Anthropogeography - Arctic regions - Juvenile literature. I. Title. II. Series: Kalman, Bobbie, 1947- . The Arctic world series.

G614.K34 1988   j913'.0911'3   LC 93-30689

350 Fifth Ave., Suite 3308
New York,
N.Y. 10118

360 York Road, R.R.4,
Niagara-on-the-Lake,
Ontario L0S 1J0

73 Lime Walk
Headington, Oxford OX3 7AD

Contents

At the top of the world

The Arctic is one of the coldest places on earth. The plants, animals, and people that spend their lives in this harsh environment must cope with severe winds, freezing temperatures, and long winter months without sunshine. There is, however, another side to the Arctic. In summer the tundra bursts with color and buzzes with life. Daylight seems endless, the flowers bloom, birds flock, and animals enjoy the bountiful feast that the sea and tundra offer.

The Arctic is a land of extremes: endless winter darkness and continuous summer daylight; ice fields and sparkling ponds; mountain peaks and rolling plains; snowy deserts and colorful tundra vegetation. At times the Arctic may be harsh, challenging, dark, and bleak, but its astounding beauty is an eternal attraction to those who visit or live there. Discover this land of surprises with us!

Where is the Arctic?

Everyone agrees that the northernmost point of the Arctic is the North Pole, but where is its southernmost boundary? Some scientists use the Arctic Circle as the boundary line, while others feel that the tree line is its natural border. There are even some areas south of both the Arctic Circle and the tree line that are considered part of the Arctic because of their extremely cold climates.

The Arctic Circle

Look at the map on the opposite page. It shows the top of the earth. The lines drawn west to east around the earth are called lines of latitude. Latitudinal lines help measure the distances north and south of the equator. Find the circle with the broken line above 60° latitude. It is the Arctic Circle.

Only dwarf trees grow along the width of the tree line.

If you lived anywhere along or above the Arctic Circle, you would experience two special days every year. One of these days falls on or around December 21. It is the winter solstice. On this day you would wake up and find that there is no daylight at all. The other special day, the summer solstice, falls on or around June 21. On this day you would go to bed, but it would stay light. These two days are the shortest and longest days of the year. Above the Arctic Circle the sun never rises on the winter solstice and never sets on the summer solstice. Because of these occurrences, some people think that the Arctic Circle should represent the southern boundary of the Arctic.

The tree line

Perhaps the most accurate southern boundary of the Arctic is the tree line. The tree line is not really a line at all, but a band of trees several kilometers wide. As you cross the width of this band, the trees become smaller and they grow farther apart. The ground underneath the trees is permanently frozen with just a thin layer of unfrozen soil on top. Only dwarf trees with short roots survive above this permafrost.

Icy winds, lack of moisture, and an even thinner layer of soil above the permafrost prevent trees from growing at all north of the tree line. Where the trees disappear, the tundra begins. Tundra is barren land with no trees or tall plants.

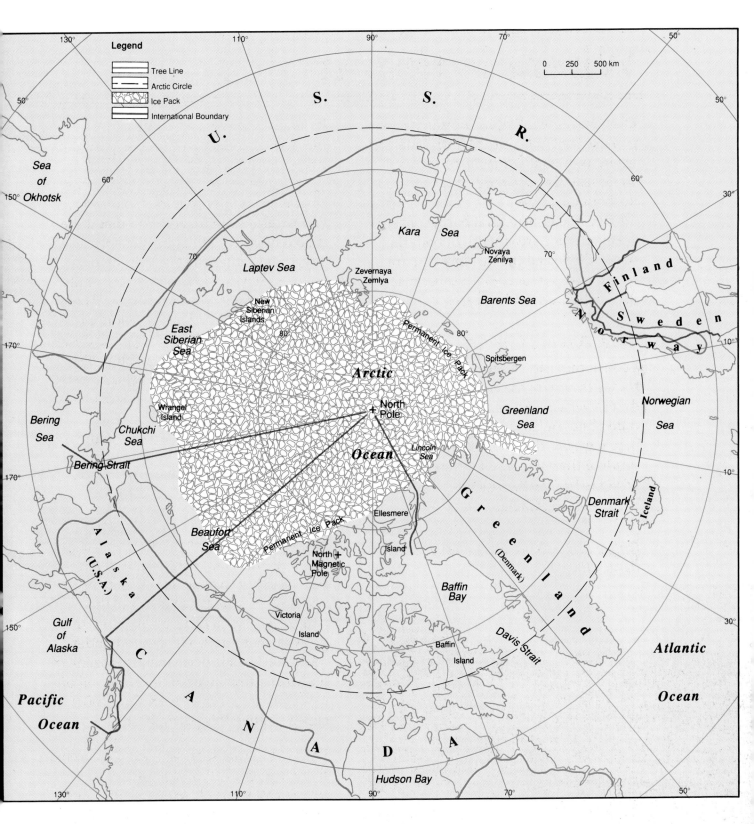

If you were to stand in this barren land without trees, you would soon notice how different it is from regions farther south. The flatness of the landscape, the frozen ground, and the darkness of the northern winter would make you aware that you were visiting one of the coldest places on earth—the Arctic.

The two north poles

Did you know that there are two north poles in the Arctic? One is called the True North Pole, and the other is the Magnetic North Pole. There are two North Poles because the earth has both a geometric axis and a magnetic axis. These axes are imaginary lines that run through the center of the earth.

The True North Pole

The earth rotates on its geometric axis. The place where the geometric axis meets the north end of the earth is known as the True North Pole. It is in the Arctic Ocean at a spot that is always covered by ice. The earth wobbles very slightly as it rotates. As a result of this wobble, the Pole actually moves a little bit from year to year. However, it never moves beyond an area about twenty meters wide, called the Chandler Circle.

The Magnetic North Pole

The Magnetic North Pole is more than 1000 kilometers from the True North Pole. It marks the top of the earth's magnetic axis. Imagine a large bar magnet running through the earth. This magnetic bar does not extend through the earth's exact middle but is a little bit off center. One end of this magnet is the Magnetic South Pole, and the other is the Magnetic North Pole. The Magnetic North Pole is located among the arctic islands of Canada.

In quest of the North Pole

People in the past were fascinated by the North Pole, and many dreamed about being the first non-native person to reach it. One of the early explorers who made several attempts to reach the North Pole was an Englishman named John Ross. On his first voyage his boat got stuck for four years in the ice around Greenland. With the help of a group of Greenlanders, called Polar Eskimos, he was able to stay alive and return home to England.

This experience did not stop him from trying again, however. On one of his expeditions into the sea around Greenland, John Ross took his nephew James Clark Ross with him. James Ross discovered something very important during this trip. As he was sailing among the northern islands of Canada, his compass began acting strangely. Instead of pointing north, it began spinning because he was surrounded by the magnetic field of the north. James Clark Ross had discovered the Magnetic North Pole!

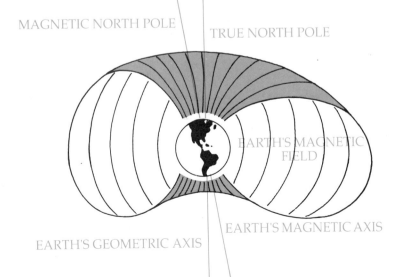

MAGNETIC NORTH POLE   TRUE NORTH POLE

EARTH'S MAGNETIC FIELD

EARTH'S MAGNETIC AXIS

EARTH'S GEOMETRIC AXIS

The "silly season" is here!

It was not until 1909 that explorers reached the True North Pole. In that year two Americans, Robert E. Peary and Matthew Henson, arrived there by sled after seven failed attempts! Since then hundreds of adventurers from all over the world have tried to reach the North Pole.

Each year, when the sun returns to the Arctic, there are always a few people who want to make their way to the North Pole. They try to reach it by dog sled, airplane, helicopter, skis, and even by motorcycle. Because few are prepared for the dangers of the Arctic, most have to be rescued. Blizzards, shifting ice, and dangerous polar bears are just some of the obstacles. However, there are always a few enthusiasts who are ready to overcome all the odds. The inhabitants of the Arctic call this eight-week run to the North Pole the "silly season" because they can't understand why people try so many silly ways to reach a place in the middle of nowhere!

9

Why is the Arctic so cold?

The farther north you go, the less heat the sun provides. Near the equator the sun's rays hit the earth straight on but, in the Arctic, the sun's rays strike the earth's surface at an angle. Rays that reach the Arctic are not very intense because they do not hit the earth directly and because they cover a larger area. In southern regions the sun appears directly overhead whereas, in the Arctic, it never rises very high above the horizon. Another reason why the land never completely warms up is that the sun's rays have little chance of being absorbed into the earth. The snow and ice make a shiny, white surface that reflects the rays back into the atmosphere.

The earth's tilts

The Arctic is not only cold in winter, but also dark. The earth is tilted on its axis as it revolves around the sun. This tilt places the North Pole in darkness for nearly six months, since the sun's rays cannot reach the top of the world. Then the earth shifts and tilts in the other direction, and the North Pole is in daylight for most of the other six months. You have read that along the Arctic Circle the sun does not rise on the winter solstice and does not set on the summer solstice. As you go farther north of the Arctic Circle, the number of days of complete sunlight in summer and complete darkness in winter increases.

Adapting to the cold

The animals that live in the Arctic all year round have adapted to the severe cold. Most have a thick layer of fat under their skins that insulates them from the cold. The fat of marine mammals is called blubber. Seals, whales, and walruses all have blubber. Animals such as the arctic fox and wolf have two layers of fur to keep out the cold. Polar bears have both fat and fur. Birds, too, often have two layers of feathers to protect them from the chill.

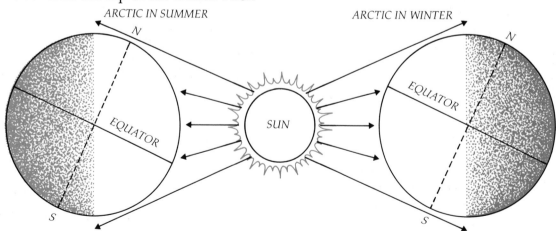

In June the Arctic is tilted towards the sun and there is sunshine 24 hours a day. In December the Antarctic is tilted towards the sun and it receives 24 hours of sunlight. At the other end of the earth, the Arctic is in total darkness.

Nothing keeps out the cold as well as fur clothing!

Lots of layers

How do people cope with the bitter cold? Native peoples of the arctic regions used to make their clothes from the hides of animals. Parkas and pants were made from caribou, fox, and wolf. Mittens and boots were fashioned from sealskin. Inner layers of clothing were of softer fur and were worn with the fur facing inward. The outer garments were often made of caribou hide and were worn with the fur facing outward. Seams were finely stitched to make the garments waterproof. Some people still wear the traditional clothing, but most buy winter clothes made of synthetic materials.

The seasons of the Arctic

The longest season in the Arctic is winter, which lasts about nine months. It is easy to tell that winter has arrived because it is dark outside for most of the day and night. Howling winds blow the snow from place to place and pile it into drifts. Sudden blizzards make it impossible to see. The average winter temperature is -30°C. It is so cold that people's breath steams and freezes in the air and, because it is dark, the weather seems even more chilling.

The first sign of spring

When the sun first begins to reappear in the far north, it is only as a slight brightening of the sky around noon. Each day this period of light lasts a little longer until the day arrives when the sun peeks above the horizon in the southern sky. Every day the sun rises higher and higher above the horizon as winter brightens into spring.

Summer is finally here!

Throughout summer the sun circles the horizon without setting. For this reason the Arctic is known as "the land of the midnight sun." Although the temperature rises only slightly above 0°C, the Arctic does have several weeks of relatively warm weather, cloudless skies, and continuous sunshine. The land turns from barren fields of ice and snow to wildflower-filled green pastures and thousands of shimmering puddles and waterways.

Autumn colors

Summer lasts approximately eight weeks. At its end the colors of the plants transform from the yellows, whites, and purples of blooming petals into the burgundy reds, golden yellows, and deep browns of autumn vegetation. As the sun sinks lower and lower in the sky each day, autumn comes to an end. The sky dims and the hard frost seals the land once more. The Arctic enters another winter of chilling darkness.

The tundra blooms with vibrant colors in the summer and early fall.

Who lives in the Arctic?

The Arctic is not one big country but the northern part of seven different countries: Canada, the United States, Greenland, Norway, Sweden, Finland, and the U.S.S.R. Many native peoples live in the arctic regions of these countries. They inhabited these regions before other people lived there. If you were to travel around the circumpolar Arctic, you would meet native peoples called Inuit, Yupik, Inupiat, Inuvialuit, Dene, Nenets, Yakut, Chukchi, Saami, and Khanti—to name a few.

A native boy from Old Crow in the North-west Territories enjoys a game of baseball.

Many Saami still herd reindeer for a living.

14

What's in a name?

In many cases the arctic native peoples refer to themselves by one name and are known to others by a different one. The people of Lapland, for example, are known as Lapps or Laplanders but refer to themselves as Saami.

"The people"

The natives who live on the coasts of Canada, Alaska, Greenland, and the U.S.S.R. are often called Eskimos. Eskimo means "eater of raw flesh." Although this name is sometimes still used, it is not the name the natives call themselves. Inuit is preferred by the people living in the eastern Canadian Arctic and in Greenland. The Mackenzie Delta people call themselves Inuvialuit. The dwellers of the Bering Sea prefer Yupik, while the North Slope Alaskans refer to themselves as Inupiat. All these names mean "the people." Although the name Inuit is used to describe a particular group of native peoples, it is also the general name used for those who were formerly known as Eskimos.

Modern or traditional?

Although arctic native peoples own television sets, speedboats, and snowmobiles, they also realize the importance of maintaining their traditional ways of life. In many arctic communities village elders are teaching classes in traditional sewing, sled building, and tool making. They are also encouraging young people to learn their native languages so that the community will not lose its rich heritage. Young adults are learning how to hunt and trap so they will not have to depend as much on highly priced imported foods.

Many Inuit use skidoos as their main means of transportation.

The Canadian Arctic

The Yukon and the Northwest Territories make up about one third of the total area of Canada. Their northern regions are above the tree line. A large part of these territories consists of islands. A group of islands is called an archipelago. The Canadian arctic archipelago has fourteen bigger islands and many smaller ones. The largest is Baffin Island. Some of the others are Victoria, Devon, Banks, and Ellesmere. The sea around these islands is covered with ice for nine months of the year.

Where do people live?

Canadians living in the north are the Inuit and many groups of Indians, such as Metis, Cree, and Dene. They live in cities, towns, villages, hamlets, and other smaller settlements. Yellowknife and Whitehorse are the two largest cities, but the towns of Iqaluit (Frobisher Bay), Fort Smith, Inuvik, and Dawson City are fairly populated.

Besides the native residents, non-native people also live and work in the north. They are employed in many of the same occupations as those of the native peoples.

The Inuit

There are about 100 000 Inuit (including Inuvialuit, Inupiat, and Yupik) in all of the arctic regions, and about 25 000 of them live in Canada. These native peoples belong to eight different tribes and speak dialects of a language called Inuktitut.

In the past the Inuit were hunters and gatherers. They lived near the coasts in camp communities during the summer and traveled and hunted together the rest of the year. The caribou, seal, polar bear, and various types of whales provided them with food, shelter, clothing, weapons, and tools. Many Inuit still hunt and fish for part of the year but maintain other jobs as well. They live and work in permanent communities but go on regular hunting and trapping excursions.

The traditional way of life is an important part of school curriculum in the far north.

16

Most northern communities are a mixture of Inuit, Dene, and non-native Canadians.

The chart in this picture shows some sounds and words in the Slavey language.

The Dene

Many different tribes of Indians live in the arctic regions. There are seven tribes that speak similar Athapaskan languages: Dogrib, Chipewyan, Yellowknife, Slavey, Hare, Nahanni, and Loucheux. The word "dene" means "the people" in each of their languages.

The Dene live and work in towns and villages along the Mackenzie River Valley and on the tundra regions of the Northwest Territories. In the past they moved from place to place, hunting caribou, bear, moose, and muskox. Today the caribou continues to be their main food source.

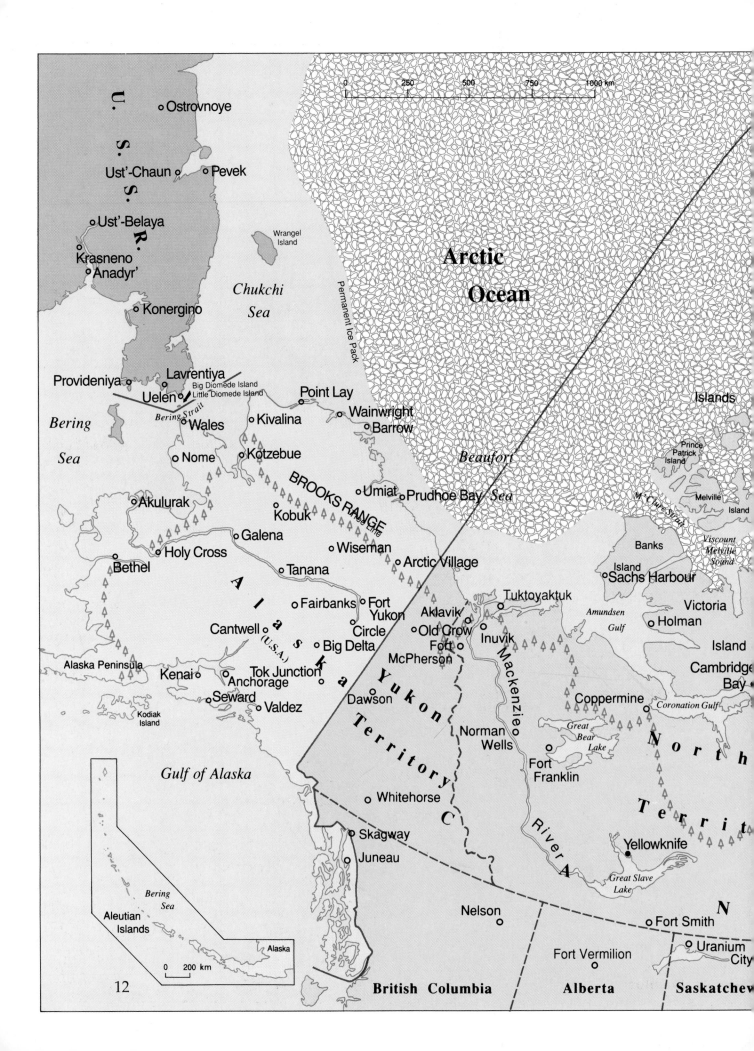

U. S. S. R.

Ostrovnoye

Ust'-Chaun   Pevek

Ust'-Belaya

Krasneno
Anadyr'

Konergino

Chukchi Sea

Wrangel Island

Arctic Ocean

Permanent Ice Pack

Islands

Providobniya

Lavrentiya
Uelen   Big Diomede Island
Little Diomede Island

Bering Strait

Point Lay

Wainwright
Barrow

Beaufort   Sea

Prince Patrick Island

Melville Island

Mc Clure Strait

Wales   Kivalina

Bering

Sea

Nome   Kotzebue

Umiat   Prudhoe Bay

Akulurak

Kobuk   BROOKS RANGE
Tree Line

Galena   Wiseman

Arctic Village

Banks
Island   Sachs Harbour

Viscount Melville Sound

Holy Cross

Tanana

Bethel

Alaska

Fairbanks   Fort Yukon

Circle

Tuktoyaktuk

Aklavik

Old Crow   Inuvik

Amundsen Gulf

Victoria
Holman

Cantwell   (U.S.A.)

Big Delta

Fort McPherson

Island

Cambridge Bay

Alaska Peninsula

Kenai   Tok Junction

Anchorage
Seward   Valdez

Dawson

Yukon

Norman Wells

Coppermine   Coronation Gulf

North

Kodiak Island

Gulf of Alaska

Territory

Great Bear Lake

Fort Franklin

T e r r i t

Whitehorse

C

Mackenzie   River   A

Yellowknife

Great Slave Lake

Skagway

Juneau

Nelson

N

Fort Smith

Bering Sea

Aleutian Islands

Alaska

0   200 km

Fort Vermilion

Uranium City

12   **British Columbia**   **Alberta**   **Saskatchew**

0   250   500   750   1000 km

North Pole

Nord

Jan Mayen Island
(Norway)

Greenland

Lincoln
Sea

Scoresbysund

Sea

Denmark
Strait

Alert

Queen

Ellesmere

G
r
e
e
n
l
a
n
d

(DENMARK)

Elizabeth

Eureka

Axel

Heiberg
Island

Island

Isachsen

Thule

Angmagsslik

North
Magnetic
Pole

Grise Fiord

Jakobshavn

Baffin

Godhavn

Disko
Bay

Bathurst
Island

Bay

Sondrestrom

Kaujuitoq
(Resolute)

Devon Island

Lancaster Sound

Davis Strait

Mittimatalik

Nuuk (Godthaab)

Julianehaab

Prince

Somerset
Island

Kangirtugaapik

of

Wales

Gulf

B
a
f
f
i
n

Island

Boothia

of

Cape
Dyer

Peninsula

Boothia

Igloolik

I
s
l
a
n
d

Pangnirtung

King
William
Island

Gjoa Haven

Foxe

Queen Maud
Gulf

Basin

Iqaluit

w   **e**   **s**   **t**

Foxe Channel

Cape
Dorset

Hudson Strait

Killiniq

Baker Lake

Southampton
Island

Kangiqsujuaq

o r i e s

Ivujivik

A

Rankin Inlet
(Kangiqtiniq)

Chesterfield
Inlet

Ungava
Bay

Kuujjuaq

D

Eskimo
Point

Tree Line

A

Hudson Bay

Inukjuak

Labrador

Churchill

an   **Manitoba**

Quebec

13

Alaska

Alaska is the largest U.S. state, but it is located far away in the northwest corner of North America. The name Alaska is an Aleut word meaning "mainland."

Who lives there?

The Yupik and Inupiat peoples of Alaska (commonly known as Eskimos), the Aleuts, and many groups of Indians are the natives of Alaska. The Eskimos live on the coastal regions, while the Tlingit, Tsimshian, Haida, and Athapaskan Indians live in the interior and south-central parts of Alaska. The Aleuts live in the Aleutians, a series of islands off the west coast.

Compared with the southern part of Alaska, few people inhabit its arctic regions. Most Alaskans live below the Arctic Circle and the tree line, in or near the coastal cities of Anchorage, Juneau, or Fairbanks. Mild weather has made Anchorage the most populated Alaskan community.

Native concerns

For a long time native Alaskans have wanted to secure their rights, manage their environment, and preserve their culture. In 1971 a new agreement was signed by native leaders and the United States Congress. It was called the Alaska Native Claims Settlement Act. Native Alaskans were given nearly a billion dollars, a lot of land, and the right to take more control of their own affairs. However, many Alaskans feel that this agreement has forced native Alaskans to give up their traditional way of life. Rapid industrial development has made it difficult for many native Alaskans to adapt. It seems that the agreement has caused more problems than it has solved.

Looking at tomorrow

To the west of mainland Alaska are two islands: Little Diomede and Big Diomede. The older people of both places remember a time when the islands were connected by a sandbar that stretched between them. Today the sandbar has disappeared. The islands have become separated and belong to two different continents. Little Diomede is part of North America, and Big Diomede is part of Eurasia. The international dateline also happens to run between these two islands so, when it is Wednesday on Little Diomede, it is Thursday on Big Diomede.

The Bering Land Bridge

Scientists believe that thousands of years ago, during the glacial ages, the level of the ocean used to be so low that a wide bridge of land almost half the width of Alaska connected the continents of North America and Eurasia. People and animals traveled across this stretch of land known as the Bering Land Bridge.

American tourists sail into Glacier Bay to get a close-up view of the spectacular glacier.

Greenland

Greenland, known as *Kalaallit Nunaat* in the Inuit language, is the biggest island in the world. It is located between Canada and Europe and is part of the North American continent. Millions of years ago it was connected to what is now Canada. Most of Greenland is covered by an enormous sheet of ice that never melts. On an island as large as Greenland the ocean's warming effect only reaches the coastal areas, leaving the rest of the island frozen.

A green land?

Why was Greenland named Greenland when it is mostly covered by ice? A Viking seafarer named Eric the Red gave Greenland its name when he sailed there in the year A.D. 982. It is possible that at the place where he landed, near Disko Bay, the land was green in the summer. However, most people think Eric chose an attractive name to encourage Norwegian settlement there. What name might have been more suitable for this island?

Nuuk, the capital city of Greenland, is also known as Godthab.

Who are the Greenlanders?

The population of Greenland is close to 50 000. Most of the inhabitants are Inuit, but there are also some Europeans. The inhabitants call themselves Greenlanders and speak Inuktitut, the Inuit language. Greenlanders live in the villages and towns of the ice-free coastal regions. The biggest town is Nuuk, with approximately 10 000 residents.

Self-government

Before 1979 Greenland was governed by Denmark. The Greenlanders, however, were not happy about being ruled from abroad. They wanted, instead, to teach their children their own native language and keep up their traditional hunting and trapping skills. Greenland became the first self-governing arctic native state. Greenlanders are in charge of their own education, language, and social programs, but Denmark retains control of Greenland's defense and foreign affairs and operates much of its commerce. Fishing is their main industry, but Greenlanders also breed sheep and hunt seals and whales.

▲ *Fiords, narrow inlets of sea between high cliffs or banks, are a familiar sight in many northern countries.*

▼ *Layers upon layers of hard ice have built up to form Greenland's ice sheet. In one spot the ice is almost three kilometers thick!*

Lapland

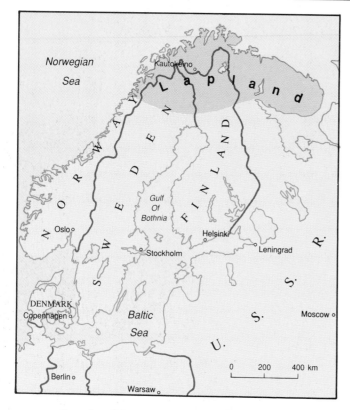

Lapland is not a country. It is a name given to describe an area that stretches across the northern regions of Norway, Sweden, Finland, and the Kola Peninsula of the U.S.S.R. The unofficial capital of Lapland is Kautokeino. The people who live in Lapland call themselves Saami.

If you were to travel across Lapland from east to west, you would first see low, flat land. This flat land consists of pastures, marshes, and forests. As you travel farther west, however, the land becomes steeper and more hilly, and soon the high peaks of the Kiolen Mountains appear on the horizon. Looking over these mountains, you would see a breathtaking view of Norway's long, narrow inlets called fiords.

Reindeer herders

You don't have to go to the North Pole to find reindeer. There are plenty of them in the north of Norway. The Lapps who live there consider the reindeer a very important source of meat and clothing. Instead of living in one place, some of these Lapps follow the migrations of the reindeer.

Unlike the caribou of North America, Lapp reindeer are tame. They are kept in herds just as cattle are, and they are used for their milk, meat, and skins.

Herding limits

Only certain Saami are allowed to own and breed reindeer. Limits have been placed on the herds in both Sweden and Norway but, in Finland, everyone may herd these animals. This traditional way of life is still followed by many Saami, although most people also work at a variety of other occupations.

The lifestyle of future generations of reindeer and their herders have been tragically affected by the nuclear disaster at Chernobyl in the U.S.S.R. The explosion let harmful materials escape into the air, and the wind carried them far and wide. Radioactive pollution traveled across eastern Europe into Scandinavia, contaminating the vegetation in its path. As a result, the meat of the reindeer that grazed on contaminated lichens is unusable for human consumption.

Saami women display their traditional boots made of reindeer skin.

Siberia

Siberia is located in the U.S.S.R. It is a huge area that occupies one third of the entire Asian continent. The name Siberia comes from "siber," a Russian word meaning "sleeping land." Sleeping land is an appropriate name for a quiet, sparsely populated place that is almost always covered in snow.

Not all of Siberia is part of the Arctic. In Siberia, as in other northern regions, there is a strip of land across the top that is known as the tundra. Below the tundra is a large forested area called the taiga. Hardy trees, such as the spruce and pine, grow on the swampy taiga. The Arctic Circle encompasses all of the tundra and the northernmost parts of the taiga.

The Siberian Arctic

You may have noticed that when you go outside on a cold winter's day, you can see your breath—but have you ever seen your breath turn into ice crystals? In the Siberian Arctic it is sometimes so cold that a person's breath turns into crystals of ice in mid-air. It isn't easy living in a place where the temperature often drops below -40°C.

Native people and hunting

There are many different native groups that live in the Siberian Arctic. Among these are the Evenks, Yakuts, Nenets, and the Chukchi. The Chukchi, who are closely related to the Inuit in their appearance and culture, live in the most northeastern part of Siberia and speak a language that is similar to Inuktitut, the language of the Inuit. There are two groups of Chukchi: the maritime Chukchi and the reindeer Chukchi.

Survival near the sea

The maritime Chukchi are closely tied to the sea and its animals. They live on the coasts of the Arctic Ocean and the Bering Strait. They are hunters of walrus, seals, and whales.

◀ *Siberian houses must be well insulated to protect the inhabitants from freezing temperatures.*

▶ *A Chukchi child dressed in a reindeer outfit goes outside to play.*

Follow those reindeer!

The reindeer Chukchi have been herding reindeer for hundreds of years longer than the Saami. Unlike Lapp reindeer, however, the reindeer that the Chukchi herd are not tame. These wild reindeer are constantly on the move in search of food, and the Chukchi follow them. After herding and lassoing the reindeer, they kill the animals for their meat and pelts. They then sell the fresh meat to the people of the nearby towns who prefer it to frozen meat from the south. The reindeer herders travel in families and live in tents called *yarangas*.

The Arctic Ocean

Millions of years ago North America, Asia, and Europe were all joined as one huge continent called Pangaea. Over a long period of time Pangaea began to break apart in the area around the Arctic. Hot rock inside the earth pushed up the land and caused the earth's crust to crack. These cracks in the earth's surface formed deep basins, which eventually filled up with water. The Arctic Ocean developed from these basins. Cracks, called ridges, can still be seen on the ocean floor.

Thousands of islands

During the break-up of Pangaea thousands of arctic islands were formed. The waterways among these islands are called straits and channels. For most of the year they are clogged with floating frozen sheets called ice floes.

Warm currents

Most of the Arctic Ocean is covered all year round by a thick layer of ice. During the spring and summer, however, some areas on the fringes of the ocean become ice free. When the weather gets warmer, the floes begin to break up in the Chukchi, Laptev, East Siberian, and Beaufort seas. Powerful ships, called icebreakers, also help break up ice in order to clear passageways for other ships.

Even though the Arctic Ocean is cold, it has warm currents, too. Warm water from a branch of the Gulf Stream in the Atlantic Ocean meets the polar water between Greenland and Spitsbergen. This warm current prevents the Norwegian and Barents seas from ever freezing over.

Warm currents keep the Norwegian Sea ice free.

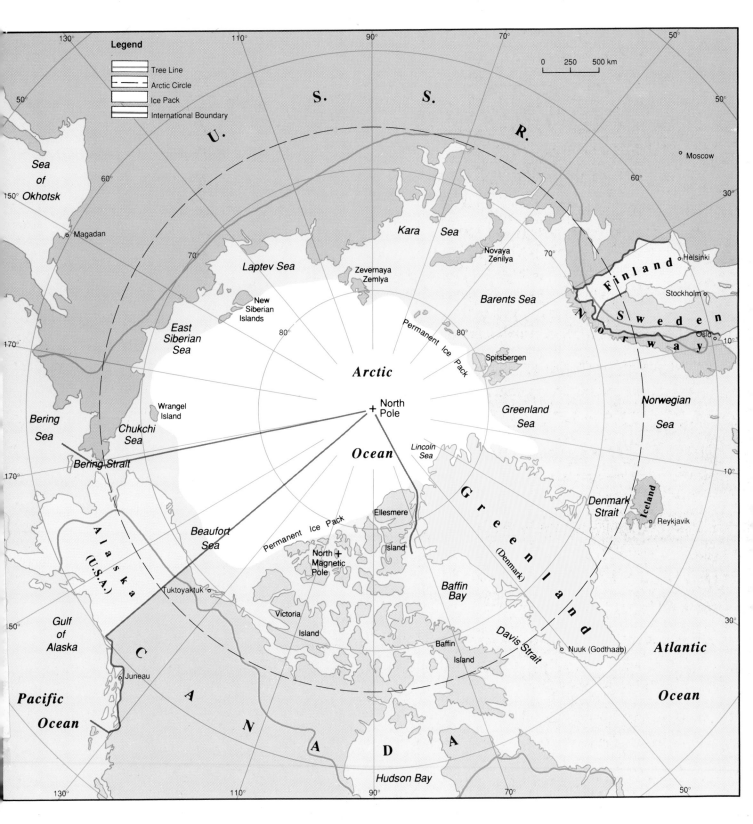

Effects on world weather

Weather forecasters broadcasting to areas south of the Arctic sometimes blame cold temperatures on arctic air masses. They are right! Cold air moving from the Arctic creates cold winds that cause temperatures to drop in areas farther south. The icy water in the Arctic Ocean also affects world weather. When cold ocean currents flow out of the north past southern land masses, they cool down the land.

29

Sea ice

How is sea ice different from the freshwater ice we use for ice cubes? The sea ice that forms on the Arctic Ocean has a high salt content. Salty ice freezes at a lower temperature than freshwater ice and, when it freezes, it looks gray and murky. After a year sea ice becomes harder and more crystal blue. (See picture on page 23.) The salt that used to be in the top layers of the ice has drained away. After summer melting and winter refreezing the small granules of salt sink to the lower layers.

All kinds of ice

People who have spent time in the Arctic know that the simple term "sea ice" cannot describe the many different forms of ice that cover the arctic waters. Sea ice is forever changing, and many words and phrases have developed to describe its different movements and formations. Here is a list of some types of ice you might find in the Arctic:

FIRST-YEAR ICE	ROUNDED ICE
SECOND-YEAR ICE	WINTER ICE
SCULPTED ICE	SLUSH ICE
CANDLE ICE	RAFTED ICE
HONEYCOMBED ICE	OLD ICE
WEATHERED ICE	BROKEN ICE
HUMMOCKED ICE	PANCAKE ICE
SUBMERGED ICE	PACK ICE
CRACKED ICE	LANDFAST ICE
ICE FLOE	ICE FIELD

Not only are there many words to describe ice, there are also several terms for snow. When the Inuit discuss snow, they use over twenty-five words. How many different types of snow can you name?

▼ *The arctic icebergs have been sculpted by wind, water, and ocean currents.*

▶ *Candle ice occurs in the springtime. When it melts, it makes a tinkling sound.*

Jumping a lead with a skidoo.

Moving and changing

In autumn the water at the edges of the Arctic Ocean starts to freeze. The ice that remains cemented to the shore is called landfast ice. Farther out to sea, where the pieces of ice called floes are constantly moving and changing, exists a region of pack ice. Sometimes pack ice covers the entire surface of the water and, at other times, there are ice-free areas called polynyas. Polynyas often form when the ice breaks up in the spring. No one is exactly sure why, but these polynyas usually appear in the same places year after year!

Ice-free pathways

Still farther out to sea the floes become more densely packed. The ice deep within the arctic ice pack is under great

Pack ice drifts with the winds, tides, and currents. Sometimes two floes ram into each other and form heaps of ice called pressure ridges. When this happens, ice often piles up underneath the water as well. These upside-down pressure ridges are called ice keels.

pressure from winds and currents. When this ice cracks, a thin, ice-free pathway of water, called a lead, sometimes develops.

A sea of pancakes

A strong wind can easily break up a thin layer of sea ice and turn it into tiny individual pieces. A breeze can cause these smaller floes to rub against one another. When their edges become rough and upturned, the sea turns into a mass of gray pancakes!

Endless fields of ice

There are some areas in the Arctic that are covered in ice all year round. This mass of sea ice, which covers the ocean at the top of the world, looks like a white field, stretching out in all directions.

Floating pieces of ice are called floes.

Pancake ice

This ice field looks like frozen land, but it is really the ice-covered Arctic Ocean.

33

The ice ages

At many different times in our planet's history, ice ages have occurred. During these ice ages the climate was so cold that any snow that fell remained. The snow accumulated over thousands of years and was compressed into rivers of ice. This ice, called a glacier, slowly moved south. Many glaciers joined to form huge sheets of ice and, ever so gradually, these ice sheets moved across the planet. The most recent ice age took place about 18 000 years ago. The ice stretched from the North Pole to below the Great Lakes! In central Europe the ice sheets stopped just short of what is now the Alps.

Hurray for interglacials!

Between ice ages there were warmer spells called interglacials. Right now we are living in an interglacial period that began 10 000 years ago. When the ice sheets melted, they left behind a changed landscape. Massive, moving ice gouged out basins and valleys. Mountain tops were ground down, and new ridges and hills formed. Rocks and boulders littered the ground as the receding glacial ice left its scars and debris on the earth's surface.

Why are there ice ages?

No one is certain why we have ice ages. Alterations in ocean currents, a shifting of the earth's axis, and a cooling of the earth's atmosphere may all be contributing causes. Variations in the activity of the sun may also alter the climate of the earth enough to bring on an ice age.

Some scientists believe that the earth is heating up. Others believe that the planet is cooling down. No one is sure about our planet's future weather patterns, but many believe that the planet will eventually cool down enough so that ice sheets will once again spread out from the Poles. No one knows when the next ice age will occur, but we hope it will not be for a long time!

▶ *(inset) A river of glacial ice makes its way to the ocean.*

▶ *As this glacier meets the ocean, huge chunks of ice crack off, or calve, to form icebergs.*

▼ *The gray shading on the map shows the maximum coverage of the ice sheets during the last ice ages.*

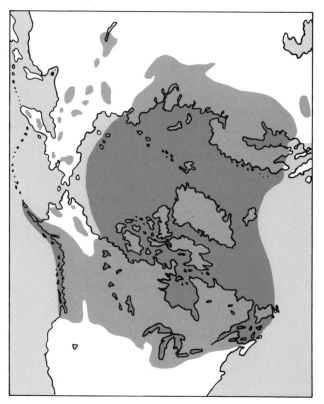

Arctic phenomena

Ice caves

Glacial ice constantly moves and changes. It carries tonnes of rock and gravel as it meanders through the landscape. Huge, wedge-shaped cracks reveal blue freshwater ice. Rivers of meltwater cut tunnels deep inside the ice. After glacial rivers have drained away, they sometimes leave huge tunnels or caves inside the glacier, such as the one in this picture. Even lakes have been known to form within glaciers!

Silent Arctic Ocean?

If you were to stand on the deck of a ship on a calm summer day, you might think that the Arctic Ocean was silent, but it isn't. A piece of equipment called a hydrophone shows that the arctic waters are very noisy indeed! The hydrophone allows people to hear underwater. If you had the use of a hydrophone, you might listen to sediments shifting or an ice keel hitting the sea floor in shallow water. Perhaps you might hear cracking sea ice or the birdlike songs of beluga whales. The hydrophone might even enable you to hear the crackling noises shrimps make when they crawl along the ocean floor!

Arctic mirages

The Arctic produces an impressive mirage called the *fata morgana*. A *fata morgana* looks like a real mountain range in the distance. It occurs when sunlight reflects off sea ice and passes through layers of warm air. The layers of air act in the same way eyeglass lenses do: they bend the light rays upward. The rays form a mountain-like image of the ice in the sky above the real ice. These mirages look so real that hundreds of explorers and surveyors have marked mountain ranges on their maps where none exist.

Depressing darkness

The long winter months of darkness can make some northern residents feel quite depressed. The Inuit word for this winter sadness is *perlerorneq*. How might constant darkness make you feel?

When icebergs melt, the sculptured shapes sometimes resemble castles or creatures. What does the photograph look like to you?

Icebergs

A glacier calving

As the ice on the front lip of a glacier spreads out into the sea, it is no longer supported by land. An iceberg is formed when a huge piece of this ice cracks and falls off the glacier. When a large iceberg tumbles into the sea, it makes a roar that can be heard from a great distance. The birth of a new iceberg is called calving. Most of the glaciers in the Arctic come from Greenland. It is estimated that the glaciers on this island calve more than 40 000 icebergs every year!

Only a small part of a floating iceberg sticks up above the water. If an iceberg is 50 meters above the surface of the water, it is 350 meters below the surface. Huge, ten-storey arctic icebergs are rare, but smaller house-sized chunks, called "bergy bits," are frequently spotted. Car-sized icebergs called "growlers" are also common.

Danger on the seas!

People aboard ships have good reason to be afraid of icebergs. Icebergs are as hard as steel and could easily topple an oil rig or tear open a ship. An arctic iceberg that drifted into the Atlantic was responsible for one of the greatest marine disasters in history.

On its maiden voyage in 1912 the *Titanic*, a British passenger liner, sank in the icy waters of the Atlantic Ocean after an iceberg ripped a 90-meter gash into the steel hull of this "unsinkable ship." Only 711 of the 2224 passengers survived the confusion and tragedy that followed.

Today the International Ice Patrol sails around the arctic waters looking for dangerous icebergs. When the Ice Patrol crew members see one, they chart its movement and warn other ships.

Can you tow an iceberg?

Sometimes tugboats are used to tow small icebergs away from ships and oil rigs. Strange currents caused by the ice below the water line often make this a very difficult task. Tugboat operators sometimes joke about towing icebergs, saying that they are never quite sure whether they are towing or being towed!

Towing an iceberg is a difficult task!

Permafrost

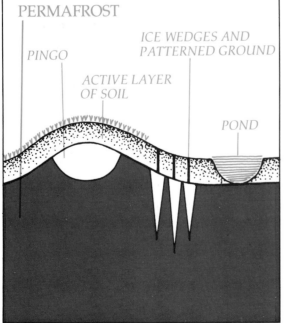

PERMAFROST

PINGO

ICE WEDGES AND
PATTERNED GROUND

ACTIVE LAYER
OF SOIL

POND

Permafrost is soil that is always frozen. It is made up of topsoil, rock, and ice. Long ago, during our earth's longest ice age, the soil froze, and parts of it still remain frozen today. Almost one quarter of the world's land is always frozen—in some places as deeply as two kilometers. Even in summer only the very top of the soil melts, and permafrost remains underneath. Although the Arctic Ocean does not freeze completely, workers on oil rigs have discovered that the ocean floor does remain permanently frozen. Like the land, it is covered with a dense layer of permafrost.

Water is transported from its source to homes in elevated, insulated pipes called utilidors.

◄ *These houses are being built on stilts so they will not melt the permafrost and sink.*

Building on stilts

Permafrost makes modern development in the Arctic difficult. Drilling in the frozen north is as hard as cutting rock. Even putting up buildings is a problem. If the buildings were constructed on the surface of the ground, the heat from inside the buildings would melt the soil. The foundations would then sink, and the buildings would collapse. Buildings must be put on stilts so their warmth does not melt the permafrost.

Don't dig!

Think of all the different things that people have buried underground: basements of houses, subways, electrical power lines, telephone cables, water

mains, and drainage pipes. In the Arctic, permafrost prevents people from putting anything underground. Sewage pipes would twist and break; water pipes would freeze solid. What other problems might permafrost cause northern residents?

Permafrost is important

Despite the many problems permafrost causes people, it is important to arctic plants and wildlife. For a few weeks in summer, as the snow and ice melt, water covers many areas of the tundra. The air is too cold for much evaporation, and the ground is frozen, so the water remains on the land. Plants, animals, and insects rely on this water for survival. If the dense layer of permafrost did not exist below the ponds and waterways, the water would seep into the ground and there would not be enough moisture to sustain life during the growing season.

Arctic landscapes

Freezing, thawing, and the shaping of the land by ice and stone has molded the Arctic into unusual landforms. It is possible to see how the ground has been changed by these elements in areas that are free of ice and snow.

The lowland Arctic

The lowland, or southern, Arctic has plains, rolling hills, and huge areas of bare rock that have been gouged by glacial ice. Frost-shattered rock on ridges and mounds of lumpy soil on slopes make walking in these areas next to impossible. The freezing and thawing of permafrost creates this lumpy soil.

The high Arctic

The northern, or high, Arctic is a mountainous, ice-capped region. Where there is no ice, the ground is barren and rocky. In some places along the coast there are huge cliffs with deep fiords. The few plants that manage to survive in the high Arctic can only grow in protected areas such as these.

Patterned ground

As the ground freezes and thaws, interesting shapes appear on the landscape. Sunken honeycomb shapes called polygons are created when the ground contracts. A polygon is a huge gouge in the earth's surface that resembles a muddy pool. Some polygons are as wide as thirty meters! Sometimes when the ground shifts, small stones and bits of gravel form raised circular outlines called tundra circles.

Pingos

One of the strangest landforms that develops on the Arctic tundra is the pingo. Pingo is the Inuit name given to huge domes of land with cores of ice. Sometimes a lake shrinks, and a thin layer of ground vegetation builds up on top of the mud-thick water. The shrunken, muddy lake becomes trapped between the quickly freezing surface soil and the permafrost below.

Streams that crisscross the tundra in summer leave interesting shapes as the ice on the bottom of their beds melts.

A pingo near Tuktoyaktuk

How pingos are formed

If you were to freeze a full bottle of water with a cork in it, the water would expand and force the cork upwards. A pingo is formed in much the same way. The trapped water freezes and pushes its way to the surface, forming a hill on the land. The earth covering the pingo prevents the ice core from melting. When wind carries away the soil on the top of the pingo, the sun melts the ice core. Pingos with melted cores look like volcanoes with huge craters. Some of the largest and oldest pingos are found in the Mackenzie Delta region of the Canadian Arctic. Some have been around for thousands of years and are as high as seventy meters! Not all pingos are old, though. Some new ones are being formed right now.

Earth hummocks

In areas where there is moisture in the ground from the summer months, frost heaves the top layer of soil into strange shapes. As a result, small mounds of soil called hummocks sometimes form on the tundra.

Earth hummocks

Arctic landscapes vary from regions of flat and barren tundra to picturesque mountainous coastal areas.

The Arctic is a cold desert

Salt-free ice is a good source of drinking water.

Most people imagine deserts as hot, sandy places, but there are also deserts in the polar regions of our earth. If an area gets less than 250 mm of rain and snow in one year, it is considered a desert. The arctic region receives as little as 125 to 200 mm of precipitation annually.

With so much snow and ice in the Arctic, it is hard to think of this place as being dry. However, very little snow actually falls and, when it does, it stays around for a long time. It only rains on rare occasions in summer. Most of the water that plants require for survival is absorbed when ice and snow melt, forming puddles and streams on top of the land. One source of fresh water for animals and people is the Arctic Ocean. Salt in the sea ice works its way down

This arctic willow's leaves are protected from the cold by small hairs.

Root systems spread out horizontally.

into the lower layers during summer thawing and winter refreezing. The top layers of sea ice are almost salt free.

Desert adaptation

Poor soil, lack of water, short summers, and low temperatures all combine to make life difficult for plants. Mosses, lichens, shrubs, grasses, and other varieties of plants grow wherever there is enough water and soil.

Root systems spread out horizontally because permafrost prevents them from growing straight down into the soil. All arctic plant life grows close to the ground, where it finds protection from the cold winds. The temperature in this blanket of vegetation at surface level is much warmer than the air a few centimeters above. Nearby rocks can also help provide heat by reflecting the sunlight and sheltering the plants from the wind.

On Baffin Island some lichens have been growing for 10 000 years.

Plant life's senior citizens

Arctic plants that survive from year to year grow very slowly. One of nature's slowest-growing plants, the lichen, can be found in the Arctic. Lichens are coarse, dry plants that cling to rocks and pockets of soil. They are well adapted to life in a harsh climate because they do not need much water and can withstand the bitter cold. They can exist for thousands of years on bare rock without any soil. Some willow and birch bushes are also very old. Scientists have counted their growing rings under a microscope and found that they have been alive for 400 years!

Hairy plants

Many arctic plants are protected from the cold air by hair! Arctic willow pods have hair on their leaves and stems to capture a warm layer of air around them. Colorful blooms also help flowers keep warm. The temperature around brightly colored flowers is several degrees higher than the temperature around flowers with white petals.

Some plants can freeze only to be completely unharmed when they thaw out.

The tundra blooms

For approximately ten months of the year arctic plants lie frozen beneath the snow. As soon as the snow melts away, sometimes before it has disappeared completely, the Arctic comes alive with color. Orange, purple, green, red, and yellow plants struggle to mature and bloom during the short growing season.

Only the hardiest plants survive an arctic summer. Icy winds sweep across the tundra, and the temperature often falls below freezing. Sometimes a snowstorm covers all the blossoming plants. Yet, despite these conditions, many kinds of plants have adapted to polar life.

caribou moss

Purple fireweed

Squirrel-tail grass

▲The colors of autumn are burgundy reds, golden yellows, and deep browns.

◄The wooly lousewort makes its own mini-climate. Its dense hairs act as insulation.

▼Arctic poppies

Cotton grass

49

Arctic resources

So far, resources such as uranium, gold, silver, copper, nickel, lead, zinc, and coal have been found in the Arctic. By far the most important North American arctic resources, however, are oil and gas.

In 1968 oil was discovered in Prudhoe Bay—a small inlet in the Beaufort Sea. Through the 1970s and into the 1980s offshore oil exploration continued despite the many costs and dangers. People in the oil and gas industries believe that there are millions of barrels of oil still to be discovered in the Arctic.

Drilling in the icy ocean

Oil companies use rigs adapted for icy waters. Some are mounted on barges or platforms and are held in place by legs of steel, cables, and a system of motors. Other types of rigs are built on their own special islands.

Drilling for oil beneath the cold waters of the Arctic Ocean is more difficult and dangerous than drilling for oil in other oceans. As the Arctic Ocean is ice-covered for most of the year, all offshore drilling must be carried out during the period of ice break-up. This makes the drilling season very short.

Transporting the fuel

Once the oil and gas have been found and taken out of the ground, they have to be shipped to the markets in the south. Pipelines and special ships called tankers are used to transport the fossil fuels. Rigs, ships, and pipelines are costly to build and maintain because they require expensive materials and a great deal of human labor.

Pipelines are built by welding sections of pipe into a continuous length. The pipeline is then coated with materials to protect it from the cold. Pumping stations along the pipeline keep the oil flowing and the pipes warm so the oil does not thicken up and stop moving. Pipelines transporting oil are kept above the ground so their warmth does not melt the permafrost. If the permafrost were to melt, the ground would become muddy and unstable, and the pipeline would sag and break.

An artificial island is constructed to support an oil rig.

The Alaskan oil pipeline

The Alaskan pipeline

Pipelines transporting oil and gas from the Arctic span thousands of kilometers. One of the longest in the Arctic—1200 kilometers—is in Alaska. In some places workers have raised the pipeline high enough to let migrating caribou pass underneath. In this way the pipeline does not prevent caribou from making their yearly journeys in search of food. Workers must be careful during construction because many animals depend on the fragile arctic vegetation, and pipeline construction could easily destroy the thin layer of ground cover that sustains plant life.

An oil worker

Dangers to the Arctic

The smallest changes can affect the food supply of the creatures that live in the Arctic. Plants and animals have a hard time finding enough food to survive even under normal conditions. When animals cannot find enough food, they die, and other animals that prey on them also die from starvation.

As more people travel and work in the Arctic, pollution increases. This is a cause for concern since the arctic environment is extremely fragile. In the Arctic, damages to the land take years to heal. For example, tire tracks made on the tundra stay there for fifty years, and garbage takes an extremely long time to decay. Unlike regions farther south, garbage in the Arctic is preserved for many years. Bacteria, which help break down many kinds of waste, do not thrive in the arctic climate.

In the Arctic, damages to the land take much longer to heal because of the cold. For example, tire tracks made on the tundra stay there for fifty years, and garbage takes forever to decay. The Arctic is much more fragile than the rest of the world.

Oil barrels litter the water and shore.

Oil spills

The danger of pollution from oil and gas spills is a serious threat to the lives of arctic plants and animals. If an oil spill from a tanker or oil rig occurred, the oil would collect in polynyas—areas of open water surrounded by ice. Polynyas are full of plankton. The fish that feed on the plankton, and the birds and animals that feed on the fish, would all be poisoned by the oil.

Air pollution

Mining and industrial manufacturing in southern cities pollutes the air. Winds carry this pollution to the Arctic. The dust of metals, such as lead and zinc, are just a few of the dangerous substances that are now destroying arctic plants. Animals browsing for food absorb these substances from the plants.

Industrial pollution

In the last thirty years oil and mining companies have been drilling and mining in the Arctic. Although these companies offer jobs to people, they also pollute the environment. Tonnes of waste results from these operations. Mine tailings, the wastes left over from mining operations, are a danger to arctic wildlife. Tailings eventually seep into the surface water—the life-giving source upon which all life depends.

Industrial accidents

The accident at the nuclear power plant in Chernobyl, U.S.S.R., contaminated many thousands of reindeer in Lapland and Siberia. No one is quite sure what lasting effects this disaster will have on life in the areas of worst contamination.

The Mackenzie Delta is one of the most unspoiled natural wildlife sanctuaries in the world. Oil exploration in the area could endanger all wildlife in the Delta.

Protecting a world treasure

Although most of the Arctic is still clean and wild, it will not stay that way for long unless people realize the value of its unspoiled state. The Arctic is a great treasure because it is one of the last areas of wilderness—and the world has just about run out of wilderness! People must make a choice between preserving this wilderness or using its valuable resources. If they choose to exploit its resources, the Arctic as we know it today may one day exist only in people's memories—or on the pages of this book!

A northern light show

Sun dogs appear on either side of the sun.

Light effects

When the sun's rays pass through the atmosphere, they produce spectacular light effects. The most common effect is the blue sky that you see every day. This effect is caused by gases and dust particles in the air playing with the sun's rays, causing us to see a blue sky! If you lived in the Arctic, other light effects, such as sun dogs and northern lights, would be common sights.

Sun dogs

Sometimes on a cold day the arctic sun shines through a thin cloud of ice crystals. The ice crystals bend the light and produce bright spots on either side of the sun. These spots are called mock suns or sun dogs. Ice crystals of different shapes cause other effects. Some ice crystals make halos appear around the sun and moon. Others form vertical beams of light called sun pillars.

Northern lights

Perhaps the most beautiful display of light in the north is the *aurora borealis*, more commonly known as the northern lights. The sky lights up with colorful curtains of white, green, blue, and purple. The Inuit and early explorers did not know what these mysterious lights were. Some were afraid of the lights, while others looked forward to seeing their breathtakingly beautiful displays.

Scientists today have discovered that the northern lights are caused by explosions on the surface of the sun. These explosions send out streams of electrical particles into space. When they reach the earth's atmosphere, the particles are attracted to the Magnetic North Pole and cause other small particles in our atmosphere to move. The energy produced by all this activity creates the *aurora borealis*.

Learn more!

The Arctic holds many mysteries and unexpected thrills worth exploring. Perhaps one day you may visit the far north or even be among the adventurers who make their way to the Pole! In the meantime find out about other fascinating aspects of the Arctic by reading about them in *The Arctic World Series*. Explore the underwater world of arctic whales as well as past and present whaling issues. Learn about the animals that make the Arctic their home. Read about life in an arctic community and find out how people in the Arctic really live. But most importantly, care about the Arctic because it belongs to you!

The midnight sun produces a spectacular light effect as it hugs the horizon.

Northern lights

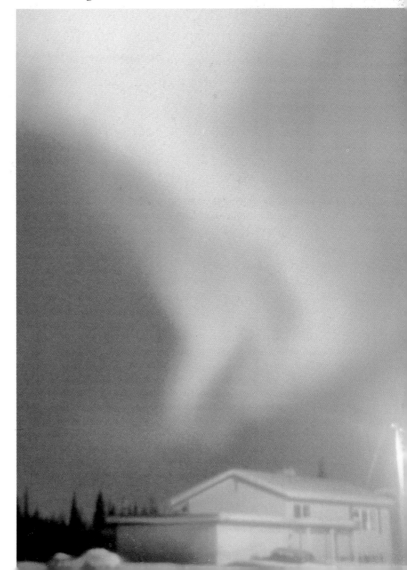

Glossary

archipelago - A large group of islands.

axis - The line around which a body, such as the earth, turns.

fiord - A narrow inlet of sea between high cliffs or banks.

frost - Water vapor that has frozen into many fine, white crystals.

glacier - Snow that accumulates over thousands of years and is compressed into rivers of ice.

ice field - A huge flat-lying plateau of glacial ice.

latitude - The distance measured in degrees north or south of the equator.

lichen - A non-flowering plant that grows close to the ground and is found in northern regions.

Mackenzie Delta - A low-lying plain situated in the western Arctic at the mouth of the Mackenzie River. It consists of lakes, ponds, and a maze of streams, and is home to millions of fish, animals, and birds.

magnetic field - The region around a magnet in which a magnetic force can be detected.

meltwater - The water that drains away from a melting glacier.

oil rig - Equipment that is used to drill into the earth to find oil.

permafrost - Soil that is always frozen.

polygon - A closed figure bounded by straight lines.

ridge - A long and narrow hill or range.

sanctuary - A place where wildlife can live safely.

solstice - Either of the two times in the year when the sun is at its farthest distance north or south of the equator. These solstices occur on or around December 21 and June 21.

taiga - Northern swampy forest.

tree line - A band of trees several kilometers wide. North of this band, no trees grow at all.

tundra - A treeless, flat region in the Arctic.

Acknowledgments

Cover photo: Barry Griffiths
Back cover photo: SSC-Photocentre-ASC/Dunkin Bancroft
Title page photo: Janet Foster/Masterfile
Photo Credits: SSC-Photocentre-ASC/Photo by: Dunkin Bancroft, pages 48(top), 48(center); Tom Bean/Masterfile, page 21; William Belsey, pages 4-5, 11; Hans Blohm/Masterfile, page 43(top); George Calef/Masterfile, pages 13, 49(top); Bruce Coleman Inc./Ned Haines/Masterfile, page 55(bottom); CSSC-Photocentre-ASC/Photo by: Judith Currelly, page 23(bottom); Esso Resources Canada Ltd., page 51(bottom); Ken Faris, pages 40(top), 41, 55(top); John Foster/Masterfile, pages 31(bottom), 32(bottom), 33(bottom left); FSSC-Photocentre-ASC/Photo by: Jean-Louis Frund, page 49(center); SSC-Photocentre-ASC/Photo by: Gabriel Gély, page 52(bottom); Barry Griffiths, pages 22, 23(top), 32(top), 42, 46(bottom); Doug Harvey, pages 33(bottom right), 35(bottom), 53; Jim Harvey, pages 6, 35 (top); Health and Welfare Canada, pages 14 (top), 15(top and bottom), 17(top), 37, 46(center), 48(bottom); HSSC-Photocentre-ASC/Photo by: Arthur Holbrook, page 33(top); Imperial Oil Limited, page 50; Margus Jukkum, Page 26; Jerome Knap, page 47(top); Tessa Macintosh/Department of Information, N.W.T. Government, pages 16, 17(bottom); SSC-Photocentre-ASC/Photo by: Peter Mackinnon, page 54; SSC-Photocentre-ASC/Photo by: Scott Miller and David Hiscocks, page 43(bottom); Clark Mishler/Masterfile, page 51(top); Mauro Morlando, pages 28, 44-45; SSC-Photocentre-ASC/Photo by: Pat Morrow, page 49(bottom left); Norwegian National Tourist Office, pages 14(bottom), 25; SSC-Photocentre- ASC/Photo by: Terry Pearce, page 46(top); SSC-Photocentre-ASC/Photo by : K-H Raach, page 12; SSC-Photocentre-ASC/Photo by: Barry Ranford, page 52(top); Wilhelm Schmidt/Masterfile, page 39; B.D. Smiley, page 47(bottom), 49(bottom right); Steve Smith/Masterfile, page 31(top).

Illustrations: Halina Below-Spada, pages 8, 10, 34, 38, 40(bottom); Brenda Clark, page 27; Tina Holdcroft, page 9.

Index

57

1415 LB Printed in the U.S.A. 98765

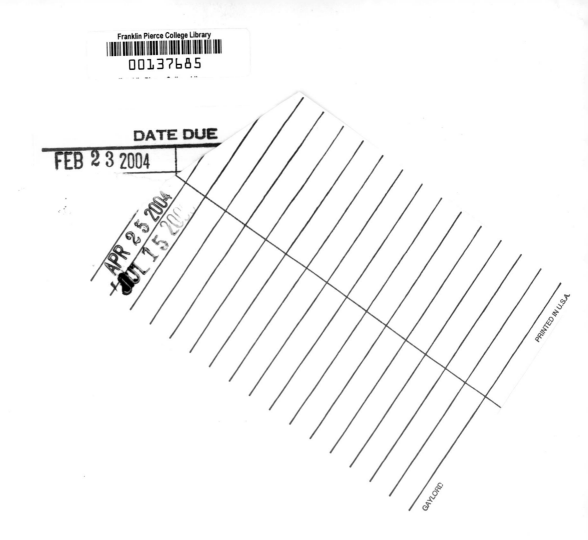